When Your Spouse Loses a Parent:
What to Say and What to Do

By Irene Rodway, JD &
Caroline Madden, MFT

TRAIN OF THOUGHT
PRESS

Publisher's Note

This book is designed to provide information and motivation to our readers. It is sold with the understanding that the publisher is not engaged to render any type of psychological, legal, or any other kind of professional advice. No warranties or guarantees are expressed or implied by the publisher's choice to include any of the content in this volume. No therapeutic relationship is established. Neither the publisher nor the individual author shall be liable for any physical, psychological, emotional, financial, or commercial damages, including, but not limited to, special, incidental, consequential, or other damages. Our views and rights are the same: You are responsible for your own choices, actions, and results.

ISBN: 978-0-9907728-3-5

Summary: How to support your spouse grieve when their parent has died.

Connie Johnston
Train of Thought Press
2275 Huntington Drive, #306
San Marino, CA 91108
Connie@TrainofThoughtPress.com
www.TrainOfThoughtPress.com

Dedication

For my loving husband, Bill.
I.R.

For my sister, Jane
C.M.

Acknowledgments

The authors would like to thank Leila Tabatabaee, PhD and Janein Chavez, MA for their professional guidance. We would also like to acknowledge the work of our editor, Rachel Mork in preparing this book for publication.

Table of Contents

Introduction

Your partner's parent recently died. You want to be supportive, but you can't figure out exactly how that support should look in practical terms. What's worse is that your spouse doesn't know what they want or need either. You want to comfort them, but you don't want to say or do anything wrong or insensitive.

Honestly, at times you feel like you don't even recognize your spouse anymore. The emotional highs and lows reveal a person you didn't know existed and sometimes don't know how to live with. Seeing your best friend and lover in so much pain leaves you feeling helpless and defeated. It doesn't have to be this way. You are in an incredibly important position and uniquely capable of helping your spouse at his or her most vulnerable time. With some guidance, you can help them through this difficult time.

You're probably wrestling with questions like: What should I say? What should I do? How long will this last? That's why I created this book – a simple guide that will teach you how to help your spouse through this grieving process, bringing you closer together at a time when many couples drift apart.

My name is Irene Rodway. I watched my late husband struggle with the loss of his mother after a long fight with Alzheimer's and then witnessed his grief when his dad died unexpectedly. Later, it was my turn to need support as I mourned the death of my mother after her prolonged illness and my father's fatal heart attack.

In addition to these experiences, I have, as a mother, watched my children go through the heartbreak of losing their beloved father and their intense grief process. They were fortunate in that they each had someone to support them. This book was inspired by the examples I witnessed as my children grieved, fully supported by their loving partners. Humbly, I recognized that although there might be "no love stronger than a mother's," partners support each other in a different, yet equally loving way.

The Loss of a Parent

Losing a parent is a once in a lifetime event that profoundly changes a person. It brings with it powerful and confusing emotions that can impact a marriage in a myriad of ways.

Losing a parent is different than other kinds of loss. To many people, it feels as though their childhood is officially over, which can be a saddening or anxiety-provoking realization. Your spouse may feel as though they have lost ties to the past, making them question their place in this world. Even though the two of you may have a family of your own, your spouse might feel as if their family "died" because the family they grew up in is forever changed. Someone they always could count on to be there is now gone forever.

Common Questions About Grief

Grief can be excruciating. Your spouse probably feels as though it will never end. Grief can change they way a person thinks, speaks and acts; it can even change some of their biological processes. This can be scary to witness – and scary to experience – making both of you wonder if your relationship will ever be the same again.

However, these changes are temporary and need to be handled carefully so that you do not shame or further upset your spouse. While there is no wrong way to mourn, there are healthy and unhealthy ways to cope with loss.

How long does grief last?
If you read medical and psychology textbooks, they will tell you that bereavement lasts up to three months. If you talk to anyone with any personal or professional experience with grief, they will tell you that although some people feel their primary phase of grief resolves within three to six months, it can take other people years to feel at peace with the loss.

What affects how quickly or slowly a person grieves the loss of a parent?
Sudden loss may elicit longer or more intense experiences of grieving for some people. This may be because, in the case of illness or another anticipated cause of death, the grieving process starts while your spouse's parent is still alive. Even though the loss was "expected," your spouse will need to feel that they are

allowed to grieve in their own time and not feel that they have a "deadline".

What are some things that commonly happen that I should attribute to the grieving process?

Your spouse may do some things that you previously would have considered unacceptable, but need to be handled with grace at this time. The following is a partial list of things that you should work to forgive:

- Forgetfulness (not filling up gas tank, losing keys, etc.)
- Crying
- Snapping
- Staring off into space
- Not being able to track your conversation
- Asking you the same question repeatedly
- Becoming disorganized or suddenly needing everything to be super organized

These sorts of changes are temporary and require patience and active forgiveness. Let your partner know that you understand and are not angry with them. A little sensitivity goes a long way to leaving your partner feeling loved and supported by you.

The Stages of Grief

I've heard about the "stages of grief." What are they? How will I know which stage my spouse is in?

Grief is often described as a series of stages. The most commonly accepted grief model was developed by Elizabeth Kübler-Ross (Kübler-Ross & Kessler, 2005). Understanding the phases of grief can help you and your spouse cope with behaviors, thoughts and anxiety that may otherwise seem random and irrational. Kübler-Ross stated that it isn't necessary for people to go through all the stages, so your spouse may only experience two or three of them. Keep in mind that not all people grieve in the same way, and that there are other feelings your spouse might have that are not listed here in this description of the typical experience of grief.

Kübler-Ross explains the process of grief as the following five stages:

- Denial
- Bargaining
- Anger
- Depression
- Acceptance

Although these are called stages, they are not always sequential or linear. Just because a person has passed through one stage, doesn't mean that they will automatically proceed into the next stage, moving forward in a predictable manner. For example, just because your spouse is no longer angry does not mean they have moved into the phase of depression. They may have moved backward into denial or bargaining. Likewise, just because a person has experienced acceptance, doesn't mean he or she won't experience a resurgence of anger or depression.

Some events are grief triggers. As you might expect, you may witness a spike of intense grieving around holidays, birthdays and rites of passage for years to come.

Understanding Stage 1: Denial & Isolation

Denial

Denial is a primary defense mechanism. In essence, your psyche tries to protect you from experiencing emotions that are too overwhelming to handle. Initially, this can be a healthy reaction – the shock and denial make it possible for a person to handle the practical responsibilities and tasks required at the time.

The underlying thought process behind denial is "this can't be happening to me." Your spouse may seek out confirmation of this. Recently bereaved people find themselves calling their parent just to chat, or thinking of things to tell their parent next time they see each other.

Denial may also serve to postpone processing grief as a way to manage lives that were chaotic or difficult even before the loss. If your spouse has a demanding career or there are children in the house, denial enables them to put off the emotional turmoil that will change life as they know it. It is normal and common for denial to last anywhere from a few weeks to a few months. Do not try to force your spouse to acknowledge the loss too soon, as it might create more pain than necessary. Grief will progress naturally.

How the denial stage may affect your marriage:
Sometimes denial manifests itself as, "I'm fine." This is especially common when the death was due to a long illness. Your spouse may tell him or herself that their parent is out of pain or that their parent wasn't "there" anyway (due to dementia, for example).

This is the type of person who may be surprised when they suddenly aren't okay a week or two after their parent's passing. They understand that they are "allowed to cry" at the funeral (if they don't hyper focus on the funeral details to distract themselves). But afterwards, they think they should be okay and able to move forward in life. They keep moving forward, doing the things they always did, but they will fail. They become puzzled because they view themselves as capable people, not fully understanding that everything isn't okay for a real and legitimate reason. Their parent died and is gone forever. It may be helpful to gently remind them that they aren't sad just because their parent died, but that the little child inside them is sad that they don't have a parent to look up to anymore.

Isolation

Denial may manifest in your marriage as temporary emotional detachment. Don't be surprised if your spouse becomes distant (isolated) during their phase of denial. Subconsciously, your spouse realizes that mourning this loss will be excruciating. By isolating and remaining in denial, they delay that experience. Your spouse may be aware that he or she can't handle grief in full force yet, and may be in denial as a form of self-protection.

They may also detach from other important emotional ties as a way to protect themselves from future grief and from confirmation that the death is real. Avoidance of family and friends can be an unconscious attempt to avoid sympathetic gestures and discussing the loss.

They will most likely also make an effort to distance themselves from those people who don't "get it." Even if you too have lost a parent, this may include you if they feel that you don't understand the grief they are experiencing.

I will give you an analogy you will understand if you are a parent. When you first became a parent, it was difficult to be around your childless friends, right? They didn't "get" the world you now occupied. You couldn't do things spur of the moment. You couldn't go to as many parties. Once you became a parent, worrying and thinking about your child was always at the back of your mind. And be honest: you couldn't deal with your childless friends talking about "how tired" or "how busy" they were. Right? They had no clue how different your world had become overnight.

In this analogy, YOU are the childless friend wanting to have a good time and wondering why your friend (your spouse) isn't "fun" anymore or seems tense all the time. Just like you now can hang out with your childless friends without being angry, your spouse will come back to you.

This isolation phase may be painful for you, but please remind yourself that it is temporary. Do not try to "coax them out of it" prematurely. If you apply pressure or try to force your spouse to open up, they may require even more emotional space.

Think of your relationship as being held together by a rubber band, requiring a specific level of tension. If you pursue your spouse, insisting on closeness and demanding that they open up, your spouse will move away in order to maintain the appropriate "tension" in the relationship. If you keep pursuing, your spouse will keep distancing. However, if you allow your spouse to pull away for a short while, he or she will move closer to you and open up when the time is right.

Understanding Stage 2: Bargaining

The phase of bargaining is fraught with magical thinking and distorted thoughts. The underlying attitude is one of negotiation: "If something or someone can make my mother come back to life, I will call her every day and tell her how much I love her," or "If something can make this un-happen, I'll donate half my income to cancer research." Your spouse may also think that if they grieve hard enough or pray hard enough, they will be granted one more day or conversation with their parent. Most grieving people understand that this is irrational thinking, but that doesn't stop the thoughts from forming and the deal with God being made.

Your spouse may seek out confirmation that their parent's death is not permanent; their father is still at the nursing home or on an extended vacation where he can't be reached. This helps delay other phases of grief that may be more difficult to handle. Do not feed into this seeking of confirmation, but be careful not to judge or ridicule it, either. Allow it to happen and fade naturally.

Grieving people may cling to physical reminders of their loved one as a way to "keep their loved one alive." Your spouse may attach disproportionate value to physical reminders of their loved one, such as old shoes, clothing, toiletries and other personal items of little monetary value. Now that their parent has died, there are no more memories to be made. All that has happened in the past is all that will ever happen. Anything that the deceased has touched or interacted with might take on special meaning. This may make it difficult to go through the deceased's possessions, even if it is necessary to do so. It is not logical, but your spouse may feel that giving away their parent's possessions makes the death more permanent or implicates them in their parent's passing.

This can also lead to heated feuds between family members over items that have little actual value. Your spouse may feel the need to keep his or her father's old bowling shoes because that was an activity they enjoyed together, and yet your spouse's brother may feel the same need. You may be tempted to think these feuds are silly, but they are very real and significant to all parties involved.

If you witness your spouse engaging in seemingly ridiculous feuds with other family members (or even more emotionally charged – second or third wives or step-children or friends of the deceased), you may need to intervene. Your spouse will need you to be nonjudgmental, rational and calm, focusing on peaceful resolutions. You can suggest that decisions regarding personal property be delayed until everyone has had a chance to mourn, or encourage everyone to support one another in this difficult time.

Aim to be the sympathetic voice of reason. If you get frustrated or fear you might lose your temper, get out of the way and let the family members deal with the situation however they choose. Be sensitive to their desire to keep you out of the negotiations altogether; only get involved if you are positive everyone involved finds your presence helpful and calming.

How the bargaining stage of grief may affect your marriage:
Like all phases of grief, it is important not to interfere with your spouse's experience of bargaining. Pointing out flaws in their logic usually will not help them move to the next phase of grieving. Usually they know their thoughts are illogical and that giving away their father's razor is not the final nail on his coffin. Still, entertaining these thoughts is normal.

If you feel inclined to respond to your spouse's distorted bargaining thought, do so without passing judgment. For example, you might sigh sympathetically and say, "It would truly be a gift if you could spend one more afternoon fishing with him, wouldn't it?" This will probably be received more positively than, "You know you're not going to be able to go fishing with him again. Don't torture yourself thinking about stuff like that."

Understanding Stage 3: Anger

While anger may seem like the most simple phase of grief, it can be subtle and manifest in unexpected ways. Often people in the phase of anger have thoughts along the lines of, "Why did this happen? Whose fault is it?"

Often people who experience anger want to find someone to blame for their suffering. They may blame themselves, doctors, God or even the deceased parent for abandoning them. This is another attempt to make sense of the intense emotions your spouse feels. Your spouse tries to diffuse the pain by using logic.

How the anger stage may affect your marriage:
Anger may manifest as increased sensitivity and reactivity, undue blame or false accusations, restlessness and/or crying spells. Some people also experience anger at self. They may entertain thoughts that they were responsible for the death of their parent or that they could have prevented or delayed the death. These thoughts are usually untrue and will fade with time.

Men and women often express anger differently. This isn't because one sex is stronger or weaker than the other or because there is an inborn psychological difference. It is because girls and boys have been trained (by societal influences and expectations) to express anger in different ways.

While every person is unique and many people fall outside rigid gender norms, generally women are okay with expressing sadness and crying but uncomfortable being a "bad girl" and expressing anger. The opposite is true of men: they learn from the time they are little boys to avoid showing feminine or "weak" emotions like crying. Instead they are trained to immediately go to anger, because it feels stronger, more masculine and more productive.

Just because a person is uncomfortable expressing an emotion does not mean they do not experience it; often it "bubbles up" in an unexpected way. A woman may cry and feel numb while underneath she is angry that her life has changed. A man might snap, punch a wall or just overreact because the deep feelings of sadness leave him feeling weak or helpless.

Anger can be a frightening emotion for some people because it feels volatile, as though they are about to lose control. While it may seem counter-intuitive, your spouse may want you around more than usual to make sure they don't do anything too impulsive. This can be taxing on you, but if you are able, try to be present as often as you can. However, if you feel their anger is likely to ignite yours, proceed with caution.

Anger can be damaging to a marriage if misdirected at a spouse. If your spouse blames you or gives you the brunt of their anger, you may find it difficult to be patient and supportive. Distancing yourself for the health of your marriage is okay, so long as you make an attempt to explain to your spouse why you are doing so. Reacting in an angry way will not be helpful. Your spouse might be looking for any reason to just explode to vent it all. Given some space, a person usually gets that they overreacted and misdirected their rage.

Understanding Stage 4: Depression

It is important to understand the difference between sadness and depression. Sadness is an elicited emotion that does not persist from day to day and week to week. Depression is a sustained mental and physical experience created by brain chemistry. It alters thoughts, behaviors and physiological processes such as digestion, sleep, reflexes and even the body's ability to heal itself.

People cannot "snap out of" depression at will because it is a neurochemical problem with behavioral symptoms. Suggesting someone "snap out of" depression is akin to suggesting someone with diabetes "snap out of" the way their body manages glucose and insulin. While behavioral treatments such as exercise, nutrition and therapy may be effective in alleviating depression, it is important to approach it as one would a medical condition.

If you notice negative changes in your spouse's sleep, appetite, energy level or participation in social activities or hobbies, your spouse may be in the phase of depression. Depressed people do not always cry or exhibit typical "sad" behaviors. Often depressed people have an overwhelming sense of being tired, flat or numb. They may feel as though crying takes too much energy. They may suffer negative changes in their self-esteem or develop a distorted view of themselves. Their thoughts may become negative and self-defeating to the point where they feel there is no point in making an effort at work, at home, in your marriage or on self-improvement or even self care.

How the depression stage may affect your marriage:
You may feel like you have lost your spouse, or like your spouse is not the person you married. You may feel lonely and frustrated that your spouse is not his or her usual funny, interesting, engaged and attractive self. If you don't educate yourself about depression, you may start to have thoughts like:

- "Maybe this marriage isn't working anymore."
- "My spouse will never snap out of this, and I don't know what to do about that."
- "Maybe I need to help my spouse 'wake up' or 'get a grip'."
- "Where did that wonderful, exciting person I married go?"

You may feel your spouse is not putting effort into the maintenance of your marriage. Try to remember that they are only "giving up" temporarily, and with time, the right support and treatment, they will find motivation again. It is important not to respond to their sense of defeat by giving up on them as well. Be present, be patient and take care of yourself. All marriages ebb and flow in their emotional intimacy, and this may be the largest experience of ebbing you've had to date. Have faith that the tide will come in again.

Your responsibility, when supporting your spouse through the depression stage, is to be patient and positive. You need to realize that this stage will not last forever. It's important to remind yourself that:

- The person I fell in love with is still inside this depressed person, and that person can return, if nurtured through this phase.
- This is temporary.
- We can get through this, and by getting through this together, we can bond even more closely.
- This is the "for better or worse" I committed to when we got married.

You *can* help your spouse a lot during this phase, but unfortunately, there is no one-size-fits-all way to help your spouse overcome depression. For example, some depressed people find it helpful to be reminded that their thoughts are distorted, but not all people respond well to this. One person may find great comfort in being told, "I know you feel as though there is no point in making an effort at work because you believe you're going to get fired, but it's important to remember that you can't always believe everything you think, especially when you're grieving. Things that feel true may not always be true."

However, another individual might take offense to the same statement and shut down or lash out in response. Gauge whether or not your spouse would respond positively when deciding whether to call attention to distorted thoughts. Always approach your spouse with compassion and patience. If you are frustrated with your spouse's prolonged depression, do not give them feedback until you can be calm and gentle.

You are allowed to be happy even if your spouse isn't happy, but you need to make sure that you do not inadvertently overcompensate for their mood by being extra upbeat and positive. Depressed people may become irritated if they feel other people are being excessively positive to counteract their negativity. It is important not to downplay or ignore their experience or try to counteract their negative statements with positive ones. Doing so may make them feel alienated and misunderstood. They may then withdraw from you and others who don't "get it."

Instead, listen and reflect upon what they are saying to you. If you feel compelled to express confidence and optimism, do so on a small scale that will be easy for someone with distorted thoughts to digest: "I know it feels like this will last forever. That must be terrible. I wish I could help you feel better."

Understanding Stage 5: Acceptance

While the word "acceptance" may sound hopeful or uplifting, the experience of acceptance as a phase of grief is more of resignation than of hope. Acceptance is a welcome period of peace amidst the struggle of denial, bargaining, anger and depression.

Signs your spouse may currently be in a phase of acceptance may include:
- The ability to talk about their loss without shutting down or becoming emotional.
- The ability to work and socialize as they had previously.
- Noticeably increased energy and closeness to you.
- Re-involvement in hobbies and other leisure activities.

Acceptance may feel as though the sun has come out after a long storm; there is still damage from the wind and rain, but it is easier to move through life as you pick up the pieces.

I heard an analogy at a time when I needed assistance understanding this stage of grief that really helped me get what "acceptance" is: it's like losing your arm.

Eventually you learn how to cope without an arm, but it's not that you don't wish you still had your arm or that you aren't still coping with the loss.

How the acceptance phase may affect your marriage:
It is important not to celebrate the phase of acceptance too readily. Keep in mind that there may be periods of acceptance that fade into another phase of grief. If you celebrate your spouse's phase of acceptance voraciously, your spouse may feel guilty, ashamed or broken if they do experience another phase of anger or depression following their first phase of acceptance. The process of grieving is not linear and does not follow a predictable pattern. Simply allow the acceptance as a period of rest without calling attention to it.

Your spouse may realize, in their newfound clarity, that they did and said some harmful, embarrassing or untrue things while they grieved. Do not contribute to their shame or guilt. Instead, normalize their grief process and demonstrate forgiveness, if you can do so genuinely.

Getting Practical: Specific Actions to Take

There are multiple ways you can support your spouse, comfort them and let them know that you are right there with them. Read through the following suggestions and highlight actions you can take today. Then reread this section periodically to see if new possibilities arise as your spouse moves between the stages of grief. The actions that are most helpful today may not be the same actions that are most helpful a month from today.

Actions to take in the first couple of months:
Show up! The funeral is just the beginning.
For a month or so, be present physically as well as emotionally. Stay close to home. This is what "for better or for worse" means. This is the time to show up. This time will never come again. Your spouse will remember all the people (including you) who showed up while he or she endured perhaps the worst pain of his or her life. Show up even when they say they are "okay" because now you know they are just in denial and having a hard time dealing with reality. Skip your normal bridge game, tennis match, or pick up basketball game, even if he or she tells you to go. Say, "I don't want to go; I want to be here with you."

Offer to help or take over logistics of household responsibilities such as meals, housekeeping, childcare, transportation and management of bills. Free your spouse to focus on the death and its aftermath. However, if your spouse wants to handle specific tasks or duties on his or her own, let them. Some people find comfort in managing logistics because it gives them a sense of control.

Show that you understand the importance of honoring the deceased.
If your spouse is responsible for making funeral arrangements and related post-mortem duties, offer to spearhead those projects.

Offer to find old pictures or objects that hold sentimental value of that parent.

Ask what your spouse needs.
Sometimes their answer may be practical: "I need to take a nap," or "I need to eat something," or "I need to cry for a minute." Sometimes their answer may be impractical or emotional: "I need my mom back," or "I need to stop crying." Sometimes they may not know what they need, but being asked can be as comforting as a more concrete form of helping.

Help your spouse get time alone, if desired.
Think before inviting people to the house or scheduling too many events. Tracking conversations and trying to care about "trivial things" may be overwhelming. Hearing people complain about traffic might frustrate them, as other people get to go about their lives while your spouse literally deals with life and death.

You probably have a sense of whether your spouse is the type of person who needs comforting or to be left alone. Because this is such a unique loss, it's possible that your spouse will process their grief differently than with other losses. However, most people need at least a little private time to grieve (e.g. going to church alone or taking a bubble bath).

Again, asking what they want is the best first step. Be flexible with this. Allow them space to change their mind. At times they might want time to themselves but then feel lonely and needy. Remember, it's just a stage. Things will get better.

Honor your spouse's communication needs.
Your partner may need to talk not just about their parent, but about details of how their parent died, how they found out about the death, how their siblings reacted, etc.

On the other hand, it's important that you learn to be comfortable with periods of silence, which can be excruciating when emotions are high. The ability to sit with someone quietly when emotions are high is a valuable skill during times of grief. If you feel compelled to say something but don't know what to say, say so. Saying, "I don't know what to say. I only wish I could take away your hurt," may be tremendously comforting.

Forgive bad moods, distance, and forgetfulness.
Forgiveness does not mean you think your spouse is justified in slamming doors, snapping at you, forgetting the milk or being distant. Forgiveness means you understand your spouse is struggling to manage their emotions and that you are willing to overlook their behavior for now. It does not mean they are right and you are wrong. Resist the urge to behave similarly. They don't have a high degree of impulse control because

inside they are so sad and angry. You *do* have control. Be the bigger person.

Actions to take in the first year and beyond:
Honor your spouse's individual and unique grieving process.
Do not pressure your spouse to seek support if they don't want it. Losing a parent can be a harsh reminder of how little we can control in the world. Your spouse may need to feel he or she has more control of his or her life; let the way they seek care be one of those ways. They may not be open to external support during certain phases of their grief.

Let them decide what they need. Remind yourself that there is no wrong way to grieve. Sometimes attempted ways to cope are ineffective, but that does not make the grieving process "wrong."

Remember: it's the little things that count.
Make small gestures – these can make a world of difference for a grieving spouse.

Offering to make dinner, packing a homemade lunch for your spouse to take to work, or taking your spouse's car to have the oil changed can show your concern and care for your grieving loved one without requiring them to talk about overwhelming feelings.

Show your love through affection.
Be affectionate and expressive. Small touches or affirmations may provide great comfort.

Make it obvious that you are always open to talking about the deceased.
Talk about your spouse's parent if they want to do so. Don't avoid talking about the deceased just because you think it will upset your spouse. Your spouse will tell you if they don't want to talk.

Offer to share or listen to positive memories of your spouse's parent.

That being said, listen more than you talk. True listening is a task mastered by few. To truly listen, you must be able to stop thinking of what you want to say next. You must detach from your own opinions and thoughts.

Identify multiples avenues of support.
You will want to turn to sources of support, such as remaining family, friends, professionals and spiritual advisors or communities. However, you will need to be sensitive to the fact that what works for you and what works for your spouse may be different. Remember, there is no "right way" to grieve.

Being around loved ones can be comforting to some and stressful to others, especially if family members are also grieving. If family and friends are willing to help in ways that your spouse has stated are helpful, take advantage of their generosity. If you feel family members are increasing your spouse's stress, attempt to shield your spouse from that gently and without contributing to the anguish of their remaining parent or siblings.

Many hospice agencies offer counseling to bereaved family members, and there are many skilled therapists on insurance panels and in private practice who specialize in grief.

There are online and in-person support groups that may be helpful if your spouse is not comfortable with formal talk therapy. Many churches also offer bereavement groups. Collecting resources for your spouse is a way to show you are concerned and willing to help. We have included a list of books for further reading at the end of this guide.

Lavish your spouse with extra love.
Figure out how your spouse best receives love. For some people, time spent together makes them feel most loved. For others, talking or physically touching provides the most comfort. For others, taking care of things around the house or other logistical matters works best. Think about ways your partner will feel "seen" and comforted and make an effort in these areas. Keep in mind that the things that might be most helpful or comforting to them may not be the things you most want to do.

Things NOT to Do:
You probably have assumptions of how you should support your spouse, but those assumptions may be wrong. You also may find yourself to be weaker or more reactive than you'd like to be, and discover that you need support and guidance in order to support your partner adequately. The following actions will make the grieving process worse – for you, for your partner and for your relationship.

Cutting your spouse off when he or she starts to tell you a story you've already heard.

You may need to listen to your spouse a lot. Do NOT express impatience if your spouse needs to retell stories, talk about the death repeatedly or discuss things that happened over and over again.

Giving pat answers or cliché phrases.

Avoid clichés and telling your spouse about the deceased's wishes or sentiments. Saying, "She wouldn't want you to be sad," or "He's in a better place," undermine the raw and necessary emotions of grief. Clichés such as "God needed another angel," or "Time heals all wounds," do not provide immediate relief of suffering.

Saying "I know how you feel"

This is particularly important if you have not lost a parent. Saying you know how your spouse feels may come across as downplaying their feelings and will have the opposite effect. In fact, this could enrage your partner.

Investing in some huge gesture of love.

Avoid "big gesture" gifts and focus on small acts of comfort or love. Big gestures may overwhelm your spouse during a time when they already feel overwhelmed. Instead, try bringing your spouse a cup of tea or small pastry when they're reading, or offering to wash the window that leads to their favorite view in the house. Buying a new car or hiring a cleaning team or repainting the entire house may be too much change for a bereaved person to process alongside their loss.

Staying away from home or keeping yourself too busy.
Don't avoid your spouse because you don't know what to say. This will exacerbate their suffering. You don't have to know what to say. Just be present.

Offering unhealthy ways to cope.
Don't suggest or enable alcohol or controlled substances. Alcohol is a depressant and may facilitate or prolong the phase of depression. Gently suggest soothing alternatives. For example, offer to draw a relaxing bath for your spouse, to go for a walk or give a back rub.

Telling your spouse what to do or how to feel.
Don't offer advice. Offer options, time and a listening ear.

Deciding your spouse should be finished grieving by a certain time.
It may be frustrating for you to witness and support their struggle, but they want relief as much as you do.

Suggesting your partner see a therapist every time he or she starts talking about the death.
Do not pawn your spouse off on a grief counselor. Counseling is meant to be in addition to a bereaved person's existing social support, of which you are a critical aspect. One hour of professional support once a week is not enough space for a person to process the complex feelings of grief.

Comparing your spouse's experience to your own.
Do not expect your spouse's grief process to be like yours if you have been in their situation. Every parent-child relationship is different, so every grieving process over a

parent is different. If your spouse asks you what your experience was like, feel free to share, so long as you remind them that every loss is different.

It's important that you do not try to "trump" their experience with yours by saying things like, "It was harder on me because..." or "This should be easier for you because at least you got to..." Be careful not to judge how they are handling the loss or express that you feel you got through the experience better than they are.

Also, you might look at the things they are doing and "know" those things won't be helpful (especially while in the denial stage). But they can't be anywhere other than where they are. It doesn't matter what you say or do; they just have to walk through it.

I understand that losing your in-law may bring up your own grief of losing your parent. It is important to honor your experience. However, I respectfully suggest that you turn to your friends and family and not your spouse with these emotions. To be blunt, your spouse needs some time to be selfish, to have it be all about them. The little girl or little boy part of them just needs you to be the adult and take care of them.

This is the concept behind something that is referred to as the "Ring Theory and Kvetching Order" created by Susan Silk and Barry Goldman (2013).

To understand this theory, draw a circle. Now put your spouse's name inside that circle. Add the names of his or her immediate family, the people most directly affected by the death.

Now draw another circle around that, bigger than the first. Write the names of the people who also are grieving, but not as deeply, such as your spouse's closest friends who also knew about and cared about the person who died.

Next, draw a circle around that. Inside that circle, add the names of people who were affected by the death more than you.

Add one last ring. You are in the next outer ring, with your kids.

Ring theory dictates that the person in the center ring gets to have the sympathy. That's who gets to say that life is unfair and cry on shoulders. The person in the center of the ring gets the attention – it's their moment.

Of course, you are perfectly welcome to say those things and receive sympathy as well – but only from people outside of the ring. You cannot take away from the energy and sympathy being delivered to the person inside the ring. Hopefully other people who are also outside the ring will have the good sense to do the same thing – shower the person inside the inner rings with love and sympathy, and get their own needs met from people outside the ring for the time being.

Expressing relief that their parent is gone.
(See Ring Theory above.) Don't discuss your dislike for their parent. In-law relationships are complicated and there may be part of you that is relieved you no longer have to navigate that territory. That doesn't mean you should bring it up, as it will only contribute to the strain

on your marriage. Right now your focus needs to be on supporting your spouse, not causing additional distress.

Getting Worried: What About Our Kids?

We have children in the house. How can we best navigate the demands of parenting our own children while my spouse grieves?

Grief is a difficult process to navigate even when there are no children in the home. If you and your spouse do have children in the home, try to provide your spouse with alone time in the house when you can. As a parent, many days may feel like they are spent trying to hold things together; this task becomes exponentially more difficult during grief.

Try the following:
- Set up play dates for the children to give both you and your spouse a break.
- Take the children out for an afternoon to give your spouse time to grieve alone.
- If your spouse finds time with the children comforting, support this. He or she may want to spend more time with your children than usual as a way to protect them and soothe themselves as parents. If this is the case, join in the family time and offer suggestions for new family rituals, or enable special time for your spouse and the kids while you take care of a mundane task that needs to be done.

How should we talk to the kids about the death?

How to talk to your child about death has been the subject of many books (see reference link at the end of the book).

The following are important points:

You will need to discuss this with your spouse before you talk to the kids so you are both on the same page. You do not want to create conflict by saying different things to the children.

Talking to children about death and grief can be an uncomfortable task. Many people avoid it altogether or use vague language to "soften the blow." This is problematic for children who are too young to understand abstract concepts like death and loss and any related aspects of spirituality that may be associated with death.

The general practice among grief counselors and therapists trained in grief is to explain death and grief in concrete terms. Saying "Grandma is an angel in heaven now," or "Grandpa is sleeping forever," may be confusing to children who cannot conceptualize that heaven is not a place they can visit for the day, and may create anxiety that if they fall asleep they will stay asleep forever. However, it is important to use age appropriate language. If your child has experienced loss of a pet or loss of a treasured comfort toy or blanket, it may be helpful to draw parallels.

If you are religious, please talk to your priest, pastor, or rabbi about how your religion views death. Part of what religion does is help us make sense of the world and our place in it. Your faith will undoubtedly have rituals around death and dying.

Your most important job as co-parent is to help your child depersonalize your spouse's emotions.

Your spouse is not just unpredictable to you; your children also wonder what's happening.

Parents sometimes get overly concerned about the effect of the death and/or changes in your spouse on the children. Even if your children were close with their grandparent, the loss is different. Yes, they will be sad. Yes, they will miss their grandparent. But it is not *their* parent that they lost. What they might be most worried about is losing *you and your spouse.* They now know that parents can <u>die</u>. Young children need to be reassured that YOU and YOUR spouse aren't going anywhere. This needs to be said to them over and over again.

Maybe you've heard that kids take everything personally. Well... it's true, they do. It's important that you explain your spouse's reaction to the death to them. You can say:

- "Mom is sad and angry because she misses Grandma."
- "Dad needs some time to himself in the garage, but he loves you very much."

If you have teens living in the house, they may be able to handle abstract concepts better than younger children, and language can be tailored to their understanding. It may be helpful to explain the phases of grief to them so they can understand why your spouse is behaving differently than usual and what they can do to help. It is also important to consider that they may have their own grief process that will be different than your spouse's and challenging in its own way.

Getting Real: Questions You Might be Asking Yourself

Why has the loss of my spouse's parent impacted our relationship so much?

Think about what a parent means to a child, even an adult child. Parents have the unique position of having known us when we were vulnerable infants and children, before we learned to put up walls and present facades. They know who we were before we were self-aware enough to be anything but authentic human beings.

Our parents watched us as we emerged from childhood into adolescence, where we tried on many faces, and then evolved into adults. They watched us make good and bad choices, and shared intimate experiences with us. And through it all loved us... or we wish they did.

When a person loses a parent, they may be thinking:
- Who else knows me the way my parent once knew me?
- Do I matter this much to anyone who is currently alive?
- What does this mean for our family legacy? Who are we as a family? Do I like who we are, how we get along?
- What impact am I making with my life? Will anyone miss me when I'm gone?
- Am I living my life to the fullest? Do I have regrets about the way I'm living?

These are deep questions and tremendous losses that understandably create emotional upheaval. Change and transition can put stress on a marriage, but if handled with sincere empathy, can lead to a positive, profound deepening of emotional intimacy.

Why is my spouse so volatile? I feel like I'm walking on eggshells!

One moment your spouse may be laughing as he or she tells a funny story about their parent. The next moment they might be angry or weeping as the loss strikes through the humorous memory, much like a sucker punch to the soul.

Loss is always difficult. Loss of a job, loss of a friendship, loss of a cherished possession – loss is always painful and always unpleasant. However, bereavement over the loss of a parent is unique. It is a deep type of loss that evokes the existential questions mentioned above.

This unpredictability of grief is unsettling for everyone involved, your spouse included. Nobody likes to be at the mercy of vacillating emotions. Your spouse may be embarrassed that he or she feels out of control of the emotions, which can result in anger. Your spouse may fear appearing weak or unstable, or may be resentful that his or her world has been turned upside down but your life still chugs along, uninterrupted.

Bereavement is not like an illness where someone gradually gets better. Your spouse may have days where they are upbeat and cheerful, followed by days of anguish and sorrow. Anniversaries, birthdays, holidays and other milestones may trigger a swell of grief.

Sometimes a sudden rush of grief will arise without any obvious trigger.

My spouse is suddenly talking about making major life changes. Is this normal? They seem a bit CRAZY!

Losing a parent may create an existential awakening in an adult child. When someone you love so deeply is taken away, no matter how suddenly or slowly, the sense of loss invites a reappraisal of what you still have. It is common to reevaluate priorities, life work and future goals.

It is not uncommon for people to embark on major projects. They get a feeling of bringing something positive into the world and building something that might last. It also distracts from the overwhelming grief and gives them something to focus on besides their loss.

Examples of this include: going back to school to get a degree, home remodeling, building/creating something tangible, writing a book or wanting a career change. (The main goal of this guide is to make sure the life change isn't a new spouse!)

Another thing that can happen is that your spouse feels liberated from the expectations of their parent. Now that the parent isn't here anymore to be "disappointed," they feel free to explore new things.

What should I do?

If what your partner wants to do won't break the bank or cause a huge upheaval in your life, then give them space to do whatever it is, even if you don't understand it. Yes, it might require vast amounts of time away from you, but here is your reality: they are already mentally gone for a while. They may be unable to be present and have fun like they used to do. Grief is like a computer program running in the background. You might not see it on the surface, but underneath, it's still processing what all this means.

If your partner's new passion is going to bankrupt you or cause too much stress, then proceed gently. Remind them that professionals advise people to not make any big decisions in the first year of grieving. Whatever they are doing, it probably is to show that something good can come out of their loss and to achieve some sense of making their parent proud.

You could suggest some other ways to get the same satisfaction without causing so much turmoil. If nothing works, then ask them just to delay their project for a while. Your partner is going through stages of grief. Maybe when they have worked through this stage, the project won't be so compelling anymore.

How will my spouse's grief affect sexual intimacy in our marriage? How should I handle this?

Grief inspires an unpredictable pattern of closeness and distance between you and your spouse. At times they may isolate, but at other times they may not want to be alone. Do not expect your sexual relationship to be exempt. On top of the exhausting task of processing emotions, those emotions can cause measurable chemical changes that influence desire for sexual intimacy.

Keep in mind that not all physical touch is sexual; your spouse may have an increased need for physical closeness, yet have no desire for sexual intimacy. Others may experience sex as a needed escape from their emotions and thus try to initiate sex more often. Sometimes sex serves as a reminder that they are part of something bigger than themselves, and that everything will be okay. Try to follow your partner's lead.

As a general rule, you will want to do the following:
- Offer physical intimacy with or without sex, as needed by your spouse.
- Be willing to forgo sex for an extended period of time if your spouse experiences low libido. Remind yourself that this is temporary. Do NOT pressure your spouse to have sex if he or she does not find it helpful.
- Welcome sexual advances from your spouse. It's important not to reject your spouse if sex is healing for him or her. They feel disconnected from the world and very alone. Remember: sexual intimacy helps your body produce natural chemicals like dopamine and oxytocin, both of which will help you feel bonded as a couple and improve mood.
- If your spouse remains uninterested or overly interested in sex for an extended period of time, and you start to struggle with their low or high libido, initiate a kind, compassionate discussion about how to handle your differences in need. If the talk does not go well, consider involving a

trained therapist so this doesn't become a hurtful (instead of helpful) part of your relationship.

But I don't get why my spouse is so upset! They didn't even get along/like their parent or they barely knew each other.

Many people are confused when a spouse has a strong reaction to the death of an estranged parent or a parent with whom they had frequent conflict. Counter-intuitively, grief may be more prolonged for people who are conflicted in their feelings for their deceased parent.

Why is this so? The loss of a parent with whom your spouse had a difficult relationship may bring up guilt, anger or other complex emotions. Your spouse may feel guilty for being a "bad child," feel cheated out of resolution of past hurts or conflict, or feel guilty for not making more of an effort to mend ties.

Many people subconsciously hope that they will someday be close to their parent, even if they have never been close to them or have had an adversarial relationship with that parent their entire life. Once the parent dies, they may feel intense pain and anger that this secret desire was never realized, especially when they see close, rewarding parent-and-adult-child relationships glorified in real life and in the movies. They may feel like they have been robbed of the opportunity to make amends or gain closure.

They may also feel guilty for feeling relieved. Everyone knows they are supposed to feel saddened by death, and they may condemn themselves or fear condemnation from others if anyone suspects they feel a sense of relief.

Conflict with a deceased parent may make grief longer and more complex. Whatever your spouse's relationship with their deceased parent, it is important to acknowledge and make space for their process.

It is also important not to remind your spouse of their conflict or estrangement in an attempt to help them move through their grief process. They have not forgotten the conflict. They are most likely re-examining or re-experiencing it.

Why isn't my partner relieved? Their parent had Alzheimer's/dementia/was in pain, etc. Now that they aren't the primary caregivers, they have their life back... and we have our marriage back!
It isn't so much that they are sad that their parent died; in a way, they are upset that they are a little girl/boy who just lost her/his mommy or daddy. It is about the loss of their own specialness and a place where they didn't have to be adults.

Also, if your in-law had a condition like dementia or Alzheimer's, your spouse has been losing their parent little by little. After the death, they realize it wasn't that they were "okay" with their parent losing their minds and personalities. It's that they had no choice other than to accept each new decline in cognitive functioning. Then they got to that new normal and moved on... until the next decline, and the next.

It's similar to being in an emergency. You have to suppress all emotion until you get to safety. Then you have the luxury to reflect upon what you just endured. When you can finally relax, it hits you like a ton of bricks.

That is what is happening to your spouse. He or she begins to understand the losses they experienced. When caretaking duties and doctor's appointments are over, healthy and familiar memories of their parent start to emerge. Again, this can feel like a sucker punch to the soul.

That might surprise them, because so many people think that they were "prepared" to lose their parent. Unfortunately, a person is never prepared for a loss of this magnitude.

How can I care for myself while caring for my bereaved spouse? It feels like everything has been dumped onto me, and I don't know how long I can do this!

Supporting anyone who is struggling can be exhausting. It is important that you do not overlook your own self-care while your spouse grieves. In addition to basic hygiene, nutrition, exercise and sleep, make sure you still allot time to do things you enjoy, such as reading for pleasure, team sports, cooking or spending time with friends.

I also had a close relationship with the deceased. Should I cry in front of my spouse?

It is okay to demonstrate emotion. It's okay that your spouse knows that you are sad too. It can feel good to your spouse to know that your relationship with their mom or dad mattered to you and you miss them as well.

You don't need to try to be a pillar of strength. If you try to behave as though you have no emotions, your spouse may feel alienated, confused or alone. Worse, they might think you didn't care about their parent and that their parent didn't matter.

For some people, it is comforting to cry or express anger with a partner. Check in with your partner to see what is helpful.

The thing to keep in mind is that no matter how close you were, how many times you talked on the phone, how many separate vacations you took, no matter how much you feel like this person was your parent, they weren't. That doesn't mean you aren't hurting and in pain. It means that you can't act like you are more hurt than your spouse. You have friends and your own family to turn to. You were definitely more close to the deceased than your own family was, so turn to them to get your sympathy. (Again, review Ring Theory above.)

My spouse seems to be always sick or feeling under the weather since the death. Is this decline in health real?

Some people experience physical problems when going through grief. Fatigue, nausea, weakened immunity, weight changes, muscle pains and difficulty sleeping are all common.

Your spouse may not recognize these symptoms as physical manifestations of his or her emotional state.

While you shouldn't discourage your spouse from seeking medical care, it may be helpful to remind them that the body is often a reflection of a person's emotions.

However your spouse experiences grief, they need your support and to feel that what they are going through is a normal reaction to the loss they have experienced.

Okay, I get that my spouse is going through a lot and I should be patient and empathic. But when is it too much? When should I start worrying?

"Unresolved grief" is the term given to a person's experience of grief when it lasts longer than is average (as expected within their social and cultural environment). Cultural beliefs about grief are diverse and contribute to many widely believed myths. Many Western scientists would be quick to label grief extending longer than six months as "unresolved grief," but there is little to be gained by doing so. It may even be harmful, as this instills the false belief in the bereaved that they are broken or unable to handle loss as others do.

If your spouse takes longer than "normal" to get through the grieving period, you will be wise to offer support and understanding instead of judgment.

If AT ANY TIME your spouse suggests that they feel they want to hurt themselves, would be better off dead, or makes any allusion to possible suicide, take it **very seriously**. Contact mental health professionals to help you ensure your spouse does not try to take their own life. By calling **1-800-273-TALK_**(8255) you'll be connected to a skilled, trained counselor at a crisis center in your area, **anytime 24/7.** Their website address is: www.suicidepreventionlifeline.org. If self-harm is imminent then you should take them to the nearest psych ER or call 9-1-1.

When should I seek out professional help for myself?

If you feel you are unable to support your spouse or your spouse's grief is more than you can manage, seek professional help for yourself and for your spouse if they are willing to receive it.

You may have had a close relationship with your in-law and now grieve the loss as well. The person you normally turn to (your spouse) is emotionally unavailable and in pain.

You will also want to get help if you sense your spouse's grief adversely affects your marriage to the point where you are tempted to give up, leave, start an affair or fight with your spouse about his or her inability to move through a particular stage of grief. It's better to get help early on, before lasting damage has been inflicted upon the relationship.

Other signs that your spouse may need professional help (these are signs that your spouse may be in a deep depression):
If after the month they are:

- Unable to work
- Unable to socialize even with you, close friends, and/or their children
- Unable to maintain their personal hygiene
- Unable to get out of bed

If after 3 months they are:

- Not eating or overeating
- Can't sleep at night
- Having panic attacks
- Lack pleasure in anything (including the children)

If after 6 months they are:

- Unable to talk about their parent without crying uncontrollably
- Still having fits of uncontrollable anger
- Having problems completing assignments at work
- Using alcohol or drugs to an unsafe degree
- Negatively affecting the kids – either by emotional distance or anger

At the end of this guide you will find a website link to other resources that may help.

Patience, Patience,
& A Little More Patience!

Caring for a spouse during bereavement can be a trying time. Your best friend and support system is emotionally unavailable. You still feel the highs and lows of life and you wish you had your partner back with you.

Remember, no one wants more to be back to "normal" than your spouse does. None of their hurtful actions are intentional. Please know they are doing their best to move forward, and that they are dealing with something devastating that they've never faced before now. Their usual coping skills aren't working and they're suffering and can't find a way out of their terrible pain.

It's a good time to remember: a partnership is more than sharing in the good times. It's also helping each other. It's being a beacon of light in a lighthouse while your spouse is in rough, stormy waters. When the fair weather returns, your spouse will know that they were (understandably) self-absorbed and not there for you. The fact that you have been there and are trying IS noticed and IS appreciated. Trust me.

Being able to prove that you are someone who can really be there when times are tough is worth more than money and good looks. Money gets spent and good looks usually fade. Character and being someone who can be counted on is priceless.

Unfortunately, you too will go through this. You will have given your partner an excellent model of how to be supportive, loving and <u>patient</u>.

We wish you the best.

Irene & Caroline

References & Other Resources

Silk,S. & Goldman, B. (2013, April 07). How Not to Say the Wrong Thing. *Los Angeles Times*. Retrieved from latimes.com

Kübler-Ross, E., & Kessler, D. (2005). *On grief and grieving: Finding the meaning of grief through the five stages of loss*. New York: Scribner.

For more general information on grief, please visit my author web page for an updated list of other books on grief and other grief resources at: www.TrainofThoughtPress.com

Resources for Your Spouse

<u>The Orphaned Adult</u> by Alexander Levy
A first hand account from the author as well as others. If you would like to get a glimpse into the pain of losing your "mommy" and/or "daddy" this is it.

<u>When Parents Die: A Guide for Adults</u> by Edward Myers
A practical guide that helps normalize the intense reaction your spouse may have to the loss of a parent.

<u>Losing A Parent: Practical Help For You And Other Family Members</u> by Fiona Marshall
Offers more perspective on dealing with terminal illness and managing familial tensions after a parent's death.

<u>On Grief and Grieving: Finding the Meaning of Grief Through the Five Stages of Loss</u> by Elisabeth Kübler-Ross & David Kessler
Kübler-Ross was and is still considered the foremost expert on grief. She studied grief and developed the five-stage model. This book is about her own experience of terminal illness and reflections on her life's work as she faced her own death.

Resources for You

Helping Grieving People: When Tears Are Not Enough: A Handbook for Care Providers by J. Shep Jeffreys
Directed towards professionals working in end-of-life care environments, but contains useful information and suggestions for compassionate treatment of bereaved people.

I Never Know What to Say: How to Help Your Family and Friends Cope with Tragedy by Nina Hermann Donnelley
This book is one of the only titles directed at friends and family of bereaved people.

Life after Loss: A Practical Guide to Renewing Your Life after Experiencing Major Loss by Bob Deits
Considered standard reading by many grief counselors, this book provides concrete suggestions for managing abstract chaos.

The Courage to Grieve: Creative Living, Recovery and Growth Through Grief by Judy Tatelbaum
A more abstract, creative guide to grief that incorporates spirituality.

Books to help you talk to your children

<u>Creative Interventions for Bereaved Children</u> By Liana Lowenstein
A book of activities to help children deal with grief. Also contains theory to help the parent.

<u>The Journey Through Grief and Loss: Helping Yourself and Your Child</u>
<u>When Grief Is Shared</u> by Robert Zucker
Suggestions on how your spouse can manage their grief as well the grief your children
might also be experiencing

<u>Life and Loss: A Guide to Help Grieving Children</u> by Linda Goldman
How to help children deal with loss in productive, creative ways.

<u>Helping Children Cope with the Loss of a Loved One: A Guide for Grownups</u> by William C. Kroen
Explains how children from infancy through age 18 perceive and react to death and specific strategies for each age group.

<u>I Miss You: A First Look at Death (First Look at Books)</u>
by Pat Thomas (Author), Leslie Harker (Illustrator)
An illustrated book for young children. Explains death in an age appropriate way.

<u>The Grieving Child: A Parent's Guide</u> by Helen Fitzgerald

Offers practical, compassionate advice for helping a child cope with the death of a parent or other loved one. Tackles tough topics like murder and suicide.

<u>The Grieving Teen : A Guide for Teenagers and Their Friends</u> by Helen Fitzgerald
Written for teenagers themselves to read.

About the Authors:

Irene Rodway, JD is an author, attorney, and long-term-care advocate living in Georgia. After her husband was diagnosed with Alzheimer's, Dr. Rodway took care of him. Through this heart-breaking experience, she learned firsthand how to navigate the daunting task of how to pay for end of life care. Dr. Rodway decided to use her experience to help others by writing about end-of-life care, death and grief.

For more information, please visit her author's page http://trainofthoughtpress.com/about-irene-rodway/

Caroline Madden, MFT is a pro-marriage therapist in private practice in Los Angeles. She helps adults, both individuals and couples, have more satisfying relationships. For more information, please visit her author website: CarolineMadden.com.

More Books By Irene Rodway, JD:
How to Pay for End-of-Life Care Without Going Bankrupt (February 2015)

More Books By Caroline Madden, MFT:
How to Go From Soul Mates to Roommates in 10 Easy Steps

Fool Me Once: Should I Take My Cheating Husband Back?

After a Good Man Cheats: How to Rebuild Trust & Intimacy With Your Wife (January 2015)

Would you like a FREE eBook?

As thanks for purchasing this book, our publisher would like to send you a free eBook.
Visit their website: TrainofThoughtPress.com to pre-order your free eBook.

We hope that you found *When Your Spouse Loses a Parent: What to Say & What to Do* useful. If you did, please consider giving it a **positive review** on Amazon.

Thank you so much,
Irene Rodway, JD &
Caroline Madden, MFT

Made in the USA
Monee, IL
14 January 2021